Autumn Leaves

by
Gail Saunders-Smith

Pebble Books
an imprint of Capstone Press

1

8282

Pebble Books

Pebble Books are published by Capstone Press
818 North Willow Street, Mankato, Minnesota 56001
http://www.capstone-press.com
Copyright © 1998 by Capstone Press
All Rights Reserved • Printed in the United States of America

Library of Congress Cataloging-in-Publication Data
Saunders-Smith, Gail.
    Autumn leaves/by Gail Saunders-Smith.
        p. cm.
    Includes bibliographical references (p. 23) and index.
    Summary: Simple text and photographs present the different types and colors of leaves found in the Northern Hemisphere in autumn.
    ISBN 1-56065-586-0
    1. Leaves--Color--Juvenile literature. 2. Fall foliage--Juvenile literature. [1. Leaves. 2. Fall foliage.] I. Title.

QK649.S26 1998
581.4′8--dc21   97-29801
                                 CIP
                                 AC

Editorial Credits
Lois Wallentine, editor; Timothy Halldin and James Franklin, design; Michelle L. Norstad, photo research
Photo Credits
William D. Adams, 10
Barbara Comnes, 1, 12
Cheryl A. Ertlet, 6
International Stock/Chuck Szymanski, 20
Photo Network/Debra Conkey, 14
Photophile/Mark Keller, 18
Cheryl Richter, 8
Mark Turner, 4
Unicorn Stock/Chromosohm/Sohm, cover; Dick Young, 16

Table of Contents

4

green leaves

6

red leaves

yellow leaves

10

orange leaves

12

gold leaves

brown leaves

dead leaves

no leaves

20

winter

Words to Know

dead—no longer alive

leaves—the flat and usually green parts of a tree; leaves sometimes change colors during fall.

winter—the season between fall and spring; the weather is at its coldest.

Read More

Gamlin, Linda. *Trees.* Eyewitness Explorers. New York: Dorling Kindersley, 1993.

Johnson, Sylvia A. *How Leaves Change.* Minneapolis: Lerner Publishing Company, 1986.

Pluckrose, Henry Arthur. *Trees.* Chicago: Children's Press, 1994.

Internet Sites

Astronomy and Earth Science: Into Every Autumn, Some Leaves Must Fall
http://earthspace.net/~kmiles/dln/10-95/octleaf.html

Why Leaves Change Color
http://www.esf.edu/pubprog/brochure/leaves/leaves.htm

You Can—Leaf Colors
http://www.cincymuseum.org/beakman/leaf.htm

Note to Parents and Teachers

This caption book illustrates different colors of leaves found in autumn. The clear photographs support the beginning reader in making and maintaining the meaning of the simple text. The noun repeats on each page while the adjective changes. The structure changes on the last page where the noun changes. All changes are depicted in the photographs. Children may need assistance in using the Table of Contents, Words to Know, Read More, Internet Sites, and Index/Word List sections of the book.

Index/Word List

Word Count: 17
Early-Intervention Level: 1